Basic Techniques
Book II

by

Clifford Wright

METAMORPHOUS

PRESS

Published by

Metamorphous Press
P.O. Box 10616
Portland, Oregon 97210-0616

Library of Congress Publication Data

Wright, Cliff, 1953-
    Basic techniques II.

    Bibliography: p.
    Includes index.
    1. Neurolinguistic programming. I. Title.
II. Title: Basic techniques 2. III. Title: Basic techniques two.
RC489.N47W74   1989   158'.1   89-12089
ISBN 1-55552-005-7

Edited by Lori Stephens
Printed in U.S.A.

TABLE OF CONTENTS

Introduction   6
Tips on Using This Book   7
Assumptions of NLP   8

SENSORY ACUITY EXERCISES

Sensory Acuity - Modeling   10
Watching for Eye Accessing Cues   12
Go Inside, Develop A State of Mind   16
Backtracking   18
Chunking   20
Pure Predicates   24
Guess That System   28
How To Be Anybody You Want To Be   30
Submodalities Shift   32
Anchoring   36
Collapsing Anchors   40
Future Pace   42
Mirroring and Cross-Over Mirroring   44
Body Sculpting   46
Matching and Mismatching   48
Relevancy Challenge   50
Six Step Reframing   52
Content Reframe, Context Reframe   56
Reframing A System   58
Agreement Frame   62

Table of Contents

ADVANCED INTEGRATION EXERCISES

Kinesthetic Advisor 64
Internal Conflict Manager 66
Circle of Excellence 68
Circle of Curiosity 70
Precision Model: Language Drill 72
Metaphor 76
New Orleans Flexibility Drill #1 78
New Orleans Flexibility Drill #2 80
Developing Non-Dominant Systems 82
Double Disassociation Phobia Cure 86
Confusion Into Clarity, Doubt Into Certainty 88
The Swish Pattern 90
Experience vs. Hallucination 92
I Trust Myself 96
Change Personal History 100
Strategies 102
New Behavior Generator 103
Creating A New Part 106

THERAPEUTIC APPLICATION EXERCISES

Acting As If 110
Accessing A Drug State 112
Pattern Interruption 114
Incongruence Instead of Drugs 116
Fluff vs. Specificity 118
Traveling Story 120
Therapy by Robot 124
Glossary 126
Bibliography 128
Index 129

Introduction

I wrote this book because I wanted a single reference source for all the exercises I learned during my certification training. It was my goal to organize the learnings I had achieved in so many places: my certification workshops, the NLP books I had read, The VAK Newsletter, and my own experiences.

By far, the vast majority of this material is from the above mentioned sources. Credit is due to Richard Bandler, John Grinder, the staff of Grinder, DeLozier and Associates, The VAK Newsletter, and Steve and Connirae Andreas, among others. Thanks to Jean Gold for her notes. A few of the exercises are given explicit credit. These are singled out only because I am certain of their authorship. The rest are from indeterminate sources. So to all you indeterminate sources out there, thank you.

I wrote this book as if you had no knowledge or introduction to NLP. All terms are explained and nothing is taken for granted. This book is not intended to be a substitute for workshop experience and neither is it intended to be an introduction to NLP. The book is useful for refreshing your memory on how you got to where you are now, or for doing further exploration in a specific area of growth or in helping a friend further develop their abilities to use this important technology. Please see *Frogs Into Princes* by Bandler and Grinder for a generic introduction to the field. For a business biased introduction, see Genie Laborde's book, *Influencing With Integrity*. If your interest is in therapy, *Magic Demystified* by Lewis and Pucelik is excellent.

Please use these exercises. Expand them. Rearrange them. Make up new ones and write them down. This is the beginning of a formal catalog of NLP exercises. Nothing would thrill me more than to include your exercises in the next edition.

Thanks and enjoy.

Tips on Using This Book

Workshop training is typically done in groups of three where Person A acts naturally and Person B is practicing the exercise. The third participant, Person C, serves as a Meta-Observer. The Meta-Person's job is to keep the other two on track and to be an impartial observer-facilitator. Each participant takes a turn at each position, but you will find that valuable learning occurs in each position. Don't be bound to the workshop format. Experiment with groups of two, three or more. Also try doing some of the exercises alone. Many easily lend themselves to internal processes.

This book is arranged very loosely; introductory basic sensory acuity exercises are closer to the beginning of the book and advanced integration and therapeutic applications are toward the end. Improved sensory acuity is a goal for all of these exercises, and you will find these skills being sharpened throughout. It is recommended that you develop your ability to notice what is going on around you by completing the early exercises first. After you gain some confidence, feel free to move on to the other exercises in any order.

During my training, it became obvious that there is no wrong way to do these exercises. You may learn something different from what was intended, but you will surely learn something!

Be prepared for unexpected learnings and enjoy them!

Assumptions of NLP

These are the assumptions behind the NLP technology.

● The meaning of your communication is the response you get.

● People can change.

● People have all the resources they need to change.

● Requisite Variety: The system or person with the most behavioral flexibility will ultimately control the interaction.

● People will choose predicates as they speak which correspond to their preferred representational system at the moment they are speaking.

● Our internal parts are operating from a positive intent.

● Our internal representation of the world is not the world but only an impoverished representation. More elegantly stated, the map is not the territory.

● A person's currently used representational system can be observed directly by watching eye accessing cues.

- If you always do what you've always done, you will always get what you've always gotten.

- Genius is a series of predictable behaviors that can be broken down into component parts which can be modeled.

- There is no failure, only feedback; no mistakes, only outcomes.

- People always make the best possible choice at the time of their decision based on the resources then available.

- Ninety-three percent of communication is nonverbal.

- You can trust your unconscious.

- A knowledge of content is not required in order to facilitate behavioral changes.

- The nature of the universe is change.

Sensory Acuity - Modeling

Purpose

To teach discrimination and behavioral flexibility in three senses; visual, auditory, and kinesthetic.

Explanation

The object of the game in NLP is to influence elegantly. Influencing is absolutely dependent on rapport. Rapport is absolutely dependent on sensory acuity. By sensory acuity, I mean the ability to accurately observe what is going on around you. Thus, we begin by developing sensory acuity.

Exercise #1

1. In each of the following parts of this exercise, Person A will do something and B will model it back. Person C will assist B in modeling precisely as A originally did.

2. Visual:

   a) Person A will do something that Person B can see.
   b) Person B will reproduce the action back to A. C will act as a Meta-Observer and will aid B in reproducing the movement faithfully.

3. Auditory:

   a) Person A will generate a sound or stream of sounds to Person B.
   b) Person B will reproduce the sounds back to A. C will again act as Meta.

4. Kinesthetic:

   a) Person A will touch Person B in a non-provocative way.
   b) Person B will reproduce the touch back to A. It is difficult for the Meta-Person to be of assistance in this exercise, but stretch for it.

Note: Variations on this theme include going for pure modalities. That is, do the kinesthetic with eyes closed while humming a tune to yourself. Do the auditory with eyes closed while pinching your finger.

Watching for Eye Accessing Cues

Purpose

To familiarize yourself with representational systems and their associated eye accessing cues.

Explanation

It is widely believed that by observing the movements of a person's eyes while they think, you can determine which representational systems they are using to process their thoughts. No one is sure why eyes move in response to (or because of) thoughts, but the notion is well accepted that the eyes are a window into the thought process of an individual. With this in mind, it is important for the novice to develop the ability to carefully observe these eye accessing cues and to correlate them with the accessing of the various representational systems. The ultimate use of this ability is to develop rapport. By knowing which representational system your partner favors, you can change to meet him in that system. You will learn how to change your system in a later exercise.

Exercise #2

1. In groups of two, Person B will present a series of questions to Person A.

2. B will ask A questions in the following categories to elicit eye movements. B will observe A carefully and note where A's eyes move in response to the questions.

   a) Visual construct: "What would you look like if you had purple hair and a green beard?"

   b) Visual remembered: "What color was your third grade teacher's hair?"

   c) Auditory constructed sounds or words: "What would your mother's voice sound like if she had a Donald Duck accent?"

   d) Auditory remembered words or sounds: "Sing the national anthem to yourself."

   e) Kinesthetic feelings: "What does it feel like when you pet a lamb?"

   f) Auditory sounds or words: "Go inside and ask yourself what you want for dinner tomorrow night."

3. If you have difficulty noticing the eye movements, design questions which require deeper processing. The harder they work to bring the memory up, the more obvious the accessing cues. As your skill improves, you will notice smaller eye movements.

4. Switch roles.

5. Notice if everyone has the same access cues. Are there any differences?

Visual accessing cues for a "normally organized" right-handed person:

V^C Visual constructed images   V^R Visual remembered
(eidetic) images

(Eyes defocused and unmoving also
indicates visual accessing)

A^C Auditory constructed   A^R Auditory remembered
sounds or words   sounds or words

K Kinesthetic feelings   A Auditory sounds or words
(also smell and taste)

Go Inside, Develop a State of Mind

Purpose

You will be asked to "go inside" in many of the exercises in this book. Going inside simply means to retrieve a memory and in so doing, retrieve a state.

Explanation

The ability to develop a state of mind implies the ability to change a state of mind. Once you have mastered this ability, you need no longer fear depression, anger, or other less than resourceful states of mind. The reality is not as easy as the theory, but the better you are able to change your states, the less likely you will be in an undesirable state. You will also find this ability will facilitate your progress in using this book, because you will be able to access a learning state for the rest of this instruction.

Exercise #3

1. Determine your outcome. Why are you going inside? You will want to know what you're after while in there and when it is okay to come back out.

2. Outcome in place, turn your awareness to your inner processes. You may begin with a dialog with yourself. You may begin to see pictures or get feelings. In any case, start by turning your attention inward.

3. Once you get something, intensify it. Make it brighter, louder, or feel it more intensely. As you identify the information content, develop the state more fully by bringing in the other systems. You might use sounds that go with the state to help you see the picture. You might use the feelings you get naturally to bring up an old memory of a picture that went with those feelings in the past.

4. Continue to branch into each of the systems until a full visual, auditory and kinesthetic representation is achieved.

5. You are now in a different state than you started out in. You have just manipulated your feelings. When would this ability serve you well?

Backtracking

Purpose

To improve sensory acuity and build rapport skills.

Explanation

This exercise teaches you what to listen for and what to ignore. It is all about how to pay attention. It is a good sensory acuity builder, but an even more valuable lesson on how to communicate. You will learn which parts of spoken communication carry the message; which parts can be economized without subtracting from the message; which parts should be emphasized to maximize comprehension of the message. This is good information to know when you want to get your point across.

Exercise #4

1. A will talk to B about something he is interested in for one to two minutes.
2. B will listen with his eyes closed. When A is done with the story, B will backtrack (recite) the general content of the story to A.
3. If B is not successful, A will repeat the story again until B has success.
4. Recycle to #1 above. Have A tell another story and have B perform a different task chosen from the list below. Insert this new task in the line in #2:

   a) Listen with eyes open, backtrack general content.
   b) Listen with eyes open, backtrack three to five key words or phrases.
   c) Listen with eyes open, backtrack A's tone, tempo and volume using the general content.
   d) Listen with eyes open, backtrack A's tone, tempo and volume for three to five key words or phrases.
   e) Listen with eyes open, backtrack several of A's gestures and/or postural shifts.
   f) Listen with eyes open, replay three to five key words or phrases with their associated gestures.

Chunking

Purpose

To demonstrate the various logical levels on which we communicate.

Explanation

Have you ever been in a situation where agreement was important but elusive? It may have seemed as if you were talking with your counterpart in different languages. This has happened to everybody at one time or another. One possible problem is that you may have been talking at different levels of specificity. When you know how to identify the various logical levels of communication, you can determine when you and your sparring partner are on different levels and you can do something about it. Agreement is always possible at least on some level. For example, you might not agree on how much to sell your car for, but you can always agree that the car is red. Next try to agree that it is a pretty nice car, then move on to what the car is worth. This is a silly example, but you get the idea of working from the general to the specific when seeking agreement. This exercise will teach you how to identify which level you are on and how to switch between levels logically and smoothly.

Exercise #5

1. This exercise works best in larger groups but can be done in groups as small as two. Arrange yourselves in a circle.

2. Person A will say a word or phrase, and each person will follow with a word which must be logically connected to the preceding word. After each person says their word, they will indicate a chunking direction for the next person to follow. Chunking is the NLP word for logical relationship. The connecting may be more specific, less specific, or equally specific. To indicate chunking direction, point your finger up to indicate that you want the next person to be less specific. Point down when you want them to be more specific, and point horizontally (right or left) when you want them to be equally specific.

3. For example: Person A says "airplane" and points up. Person B must find a word which is less specific and has something to do with airplanes. They might say "vehicles" or they might say "things that fly." Now Person B indicates by finger motion a horizontal move. If Person B's word was "things that fly," Person C might respond by saying "things that swim." C has stayed at the same logical level but has moved over.

4. You continue around the circle until done.

5. Do a round where there is no limitation on chunk size.

6. Do a round where chunk size is restricted to the smallest size possible.

Chunking

7. Do a round where the words are part of a single topic. For example; all the words might have something to do with NLP, or cooking, or the universe.

8. A sample round might be as follows:

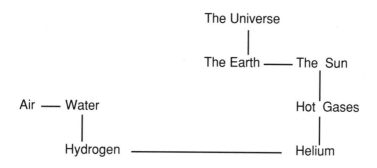

Pure Predicates

Purpose

To develop your ability to match predicates as they are spoken.

Explanation

The magic of rapport building depends on understanding and being understood. The feeling that you are being heard is critical in this endeavor. This exercise teaches the ability to identify a speaker's primary representational system through listening carefully to the predicates chosen in speech. In this way, the NLP adept can match representational systems and insure a quick and effective rapport building experience. You will learn how to observe and respond to predicates chosen by your speaking partner.

Exercise #6

1. Person A will speak with Person B about any topic he chooses.

2. A speaks in groups of three or four sentences.

3. Person B responds in context and matches the type and order of predicates.

4. For example, Person A says "I've been feeling kind of tired lately and I can't get a handle on just why. A friend pointed out that it might be that I am overextended. But something tells me that's not it."

B responds, "That's heavy, man. I can connect with that. I have friends that are always trying to show me stuff too. But I hear you when you say it must be something else."

5. Rotate after five minutes in each position.

6. A sample of predicate phrases to look for:

Visual

An eyeful
Beyond a shadow of
  a doubt
Clear-cut
Eye to eye
Get perspective on
Bring into focus
Horse of a different
  color
Make a scene
Mental picture
Naked eye
Photographic memory
Pretty as a picture
Short sighted
Sight for sore eyes
Tunnel vision
Brighten up
It's clear that
Lost/gained focus on
I get the picture

Appears to me
Bird's eye view
Catch a glimpse of
Dim view
Flashed on
Get a scope of
Hazy idea
In light of
Looks like
Mental image
Mind's eye
Paint a picture
Plainly see
See to it
Showing off
Take a peek
Up front
Project the image
Imagine this scene
Blinded by

Auditory

After-thought
Clear as a bell
Clearly expressed
Describe in detail
I'm hearing you
Give an account of
Listen to

Blabbermouth
Get clear on
Call on me
An earful
Express yourself
Give me your ear
Heard voices

Hidden message
Idle talk
Inquire into
Loud and clear
Power of speech
Outspoken
Rings a bell
Tattletale
Tongue-tied
Unheard of
Voiced an opinion
Within hearing range
Word for word
Turn up the volume

Hold your tongue
Chatting
Key note speaker
Manner of speaking
Purrs like a kitten
Rap session
State your purpose
To tell the truth
Tuned in/out
Utterly
Well informed
Ear shot
Amplify

Kinesthetic

All washed up
Chip off the old block
Control yourself
Firm foundation
Get a handle on
Get in touch with
Get your goat
Heated argument
Hold on
Hot head
Light headed
Not following you
Sharp as a tack
Smooth operator
Stiff upper lip
Too much a hassle
Underhanded
Follow train of thought
If it feels right
Too hot to handle

Boils down to
Come to grips with
Cool/calm/collected
Floating on air
Get a load of this
Get the drift of
Hand in hand
Hold it
Keep your shirt on
Lay cards on table
Moment of panic
Pull some strings
Slipped my mind
Start from scratch
Stuffed shirt
Topsy turvy
Heavy
Heavy handed
Feels good to me
Powerful feeling

Guess That System

Purpose

To identify representational systems while in use.

Explanation

The ability to identify and respond in the appropriate representational system is important when you desire to quickly build rapport. This exercise continues the teaching of identification of representational systems and is based on the fact that each representational system has a characteristic sound. The visual system tends to be higher toned, throaty or nasal and is faster in tempo. Speech in the auditory system is more mid-ranged and more melodic. It tends to be evenly paced. Kinesthetic speech patterns are deepest in tone and slowest paced.

Exercise #7

1. Person A will identify and then access a representational system (either visual, auditory or kinesthetic). He will then count out loud from 1 to 25 while keeping the chosen system as pure in type as possible. Person B will calibrate this system with the Meta's help.

2. Person A will choose a second system and count from 26 to 50. Again, Person B will calibrate to this system.

3. Finally, Person A will access the last system and count from 51 to 75.

4. Now that Person B is fully calibrated to what each representational system looks, sound and feels like to A, he will guess which system A is in:

> a) Meta-Person whispers a system type into A's ear so that B cannot hear it. B must guess which system A is using. Meta helps A to accurately reproduce the chosen system.
> b) A recites a poem or story. As it is being recited, Meta will secretly signal A so B cannot see the signal. With each signal, A will change his system and will continue in that system until B successfully identifies it.

5. Stretch. Do the same exercise but facing away from each other or with eyes closed.

How To Be Anybody You Want To Be

Purpose

To develop your sensory acuity to the point at which you can become another person. This is most easily done in groups of four.

Explanation

The Native American Indians have an old saying that goes something like this: "Before you criticize me, walk a mile in my moccasins." The application of this exercise is to teach you how to model the behavior of and then become anyone you want to become. This is a useful precursor to criticism as mentioned above, but more importantly, it is a useful way to incorporate the best behavior available to you from your universe of friends and acquaintances. This exercise is limited to modeling physiology and voice patterns, but you can expand this to include all facets of someone you would like to learn from. First get the persmission of the person you admire and respect; then model the behavior you find particularly desirable. In this way, you can evolve your personality and become anyone you want.

Exercise #8

1. Person A talks to Person B about any subject.

2. B just listens and gets into rapport with A.

3. C mimics A's body posture, breathing and even mumbles A's words quietly if this can be done without distraction.

4. D (the Meta) helps C by providing sensory specific information about A's behavior that might help C mimic A better.

5. C calibrates to A while sitting down, standing and while walking around the room. When C has a good construct of A's physiology, the fun begins.

6. C leaves the room. A talks with B about any topic. D will observe the interaction in order to evaluate C when he comes back into the room.

7. C returns. The topic is stated and C is to interact with B as if he were A. The most successful performance is where C matches the physiology of A the best. (C may talk if this helps him match physiology better.)

8. D evaluates C's performance and helps enhance it.

9. Do the same sequence of steps, but this time pay attention to voice instead of posture (or for a stretch, mimic both posture and voice). The test is having C go away and having A continue to talk to B on the same topic. After a moment away, C returns and the conversation goes back to where it was when he left. C now picks up as if he were A, matching as best he can. D helps C to stay in character.

10. At a later time, consider taking this exercise into the streets. Find someone who looks tired and model their physiology. Walk like them for a block or two. How do you feel? Now find a kid at play and model their behavior. How do you feel now? Is there a take home lesson about whom you want to associate with and model?

Submodalities Shift

Purpose

To show the effects of changing one or more submodality elements on subjective experience.

Explanation

Submodalities are the smaller parts which make up each of the three main representational systems. Vision consists of color, movement, size, shape and so on. Likewise, hearing and feeling can be broken down into smaller components. The usefulness of experimenting with submodality shifts is the effects they have on experience and, ultimately, the effects they have on changing experience. One of the most compelling of the NLP therapeutic approaches is the phobia cure. It relies heavily on changing the individual elements in our memories. By changing our representation of the thing we are afraid of, we inevitably change the fear. This is incredibly powerful. It is also a lot of fun.

Exercise #9

1. Choose a pleasant experience, go inside and get a picture or movie of it. Discover the effects of changing each of the following.

2. Visual:

>   a) color; vary the intensity of color from intense bright colors to black and white.
>   b) distance; change from very close to far away.
>   c) depth; vary the picture from a flat, two dimensional photo to the full depth of three dimensions.
>   d) duration; vary from a quick, fleeting appearance to a persistent image that stays for some time.
>   e) clarity; change the picture from crystal-clear clarity of detail to fuzzy indistinctness.
>   f) contrast; adjust the difference between light and dark, from stark contrast to more continuous gradations of gray.
>   g) scope; vary from a bounded picture within a frame to a panoramic picture that continues around behind your head, so that if you turn your head, you can see more of it.
>   h) movement; change the picture from a still photo or slide to a movie.

i) speed; adjust the speed of the movie from very slow to very fast.

j) hue; change the color balance. For example, increase the intensity of reds and decrease the blues and greens.

k) transparency; make the image transparent, so that you can see what's beneath the surface.

l) aspect ratio; make a framed picture tall and narrow and then short and wide.

m) orientation; tilt the top of that picture away from you and then toward you.

n) foreground/background; vary the difference or separation between foreground (what interests you most) and background (the context that just happens to be there). Then try reversing it, so that the background becomes interesting foreground.

o) sparkle; make individual objects in the scene sparkle.

p) strobe; make the whole picture strobe on and off. Make elements of the picture strobe.

q) direction of lighting; change the direction light comes from. Move the source and cause the shadows to change.

r) texture; change the texture of individual objects in the scene. Now change the texture of the whole picture from a glossy to a matte finish.

s) associated/disassociated; put yourself into the picture. Remove yourself from the picture.
t) number of images; split the single picture into multiple identical images. Arrange the images in a circle, a line off into infinity, or other shapes.

Experiment in the same way with each of the following:

3. Auditory:

Pitch	Volume
Timbre tonality	Duration
Figure/ground	Symmetry
Digital (words)	Distance
Clarity	Rhythm
Tempo (speed)	Location
Contrast	Resonance with
Number	Continuous or interrupted
Monaural/stereo	Associated/disassociated
Context	External/internal source

4. Kinesthetic

Pressure	Extent
Number	Shape
Movement	Texture
Duration	Frequency (tempo)
Location	Temperature
Intensity	

Anchoring

Purpose

This exercise will teach you to anchor in the visual, auditory and kinesthetic systems.

Explanation

Anchoring is the NLP name given to a powerful technique that allows you to recall on demand a full representation of any experience. The anchor can be a touch, a sound, or something seen. We each have many anchors. Some are positive and some negative; remember your favorite song from your high school days and replay it in your head. What state is recreated by the simple replaying of that song? Now remember the sight of your father's face when he was about to spank you as a child. What state does that put you into in a big hurry? These memories act as anchors for specific states that you were in when the anchors were set. Inadvertent anchors are present in everyone and were put there by the circumstances of your life.

Exercise #10

The following exercise is devoted to teaching you how to create your own anchors intentionally. You will discover the ability to make yourself smile by triggering your own anchor. When would this come in handy? The ability to change our internal state, regardless of what is happening externally, is a valuable personal resource.

1. Two people, A and B, sit facing each other and talk about any topic of interest. Person B will look for any naturally recurring behavior seen in A as he is talking.

2. Person B decides on a particular behavior which he desires to elicit. This might be a head nod, a twitch of a finger, a phrase spoken repetitively, or any other easily recognized and recurrent behavior pattern.

3. Anchor the behavior using only one of the systems for each round:

> a) visual: make a silent hand movement;
> b) auditory: make a sound without moving any part of your body;
> c) kinesthetic; touch A in an unobtrusive way (it is difficult to touch someone without it being noticed visually, but stretch for it).

Set the anchor each time you notice the behavior you wish to elicit later. Make the anchor subtle so that A does not consciously notice it but obvious enough to insure it being noticed. This takes a little practice.

Anchoring

4. Test your anchor. When A is not doing the behavior you anchored, trigger your anchor and see if you get the behavior. If you do, the anchor was well set. If not, go back and re-anchor in a more obvious and/or different way.

5. Stretch. Intensify the anchored behavior response. Think of ways to elicit a stronger-than-anchored response.

6. A fun thing you can do is test your anchor over time. Trigger it an hour after the exercise is done. Do it a day or a week later. Determine why some anchors last longer than others.

7. Criteria for anchoring:

        a) intensity or purity of experience;
        b) timing; at peak of experience;
        c) accuracy of replication of anchor.

8. Stacking Anchors; you can amplify the response you get from an anchor by a technique called stacking. Stacking anchors is when you use the same anchor repetitively to get a combination anchor which elicits several memories. The effect is additive and you can create some very powerful combination anchors in this way.

Collapsing Anchors

Purpose

To create a new experience from two separate prior experiences by the process of addition.

Explanation

Collapsing anchors is the the logical next step which follows the setting of anchors. When anchors are collapsed, you get the average of the two anchors. That is, if you have a very powerful negative anchor and a very powerful positive anchor, triggering them simultaneously will result in a single very weak anchor and the loss of each of the former powerful anchors. This is very useful for changing behavior and for minimizing the effects of negative anchors. Don't forget, however, that a positive anchor is used up in the process. Also be aware that when anchors are triggered together, their effect is in proportion to their emotional power. This process works additively. For example, you may need to stack several weak positive anchors together in order to neutralize a single very strong negative anchor.

Exercise #11

1. Person A will remember two states, one where she was wonderful and the other where she was not so wonderful.

2. B will assist B in developing a full visual, kinesthetic and auditory representation of each state and will anchor each state with a different kinesthetic anchor. Negative states are usually more powerful than positive, so it is important to stack positive anchors to insure that the positive state is the strongest. When you do the collapse, you want to be sure the positive state "wins." Use a kinesthetic anchor for this exercise. It will be easier to hold both anchors for a few minutes when they are done kinesthetically. It is somewhat more difficult to sustain the trigger when the anchor is visual or auditory.

3. Test each anchor to be sure each is fully developed and elicits the state intended.

4. Trigger both anchors simultaneously. You will see the two states flashing across her physiology. Each will compete in her consciousness. Ultimately, there will be integration. To insure the positive state's dominance in the integration, release the negative anchor moments before you release the positive. At this point, A has new choices for the next time she is faced with the same situation.

5. If the integration A achieves is not fully positive, recycle to #2 above and stack more positive anchors.

Future Pace

Purpose

Future pacing is a valuable smaller piece of many of the exercises in this book. It allows you to transfer what happens in the exercises into your "real" life in the present and near future.

Explanation

Classroom education has the possible limitation of never leaving the classroom. It is all too easy to acquire intellectual learning and have a life that is no better for it due to lack of application. The ability to future pace is very important if you are to take the lessons of the classroom from this book into your real life. By future pacing, you can see, feel, and hear your future unfolding before you. In this future projection, you can try out your knowledge and fine tune it to your preferences. In this way, integration is assured and you can relax, knowing that the behavior pattern is safely stored away, waiting for the circumstantial trigger to bring it forth.

Exercise #12

1. Person B will assist Person A in a learning. You might use one of the exercises from this book. Anchor the learned behavior in A.

2, With learning in hand, A will be instructed by B as to how to integrate this learning so that it will be available when it is required in the future. This is the future pace.

3. B asks A to: "Think of a time in the future where you would benefit from this learning." A now goes inside to sort through past experiences where this new knowledge would have been useful. In the process, A generates a possible future scenario where the new learning will be applicable.

4. B asks A to create a movie of this future situation. As A begins to run the movie, B triggers A's new learning anchor. The movie is run out in A's mind and the new behavior or learning is integrated into the process.

5. Test: Ask A to think of a different situation where this new learning would be of no use. Ask A to again run a movie of how this other future situation will look. If A plays the movie of the new situation with the new learning, future pacing has been completed. If A runs the movie and does not get a satisfactory experience of the new learning being present, recycle to #3 above and strengthen the future pace.

Mirroring and Cross-Over Mirroring

Purpose

To develop the rapport building skills of matching directly and indirectly: posture, breathing and predicates. (Note: other names for mirroring are matching or pacing.)

Explanation

We have spoken about the benefits of modeling another person's behavior in previous exercises, but what about the times when it is physically or emotionally destructive to model another person's behavior? Cross-over mirroring is very useful when rapport requires you to mirror but direct mirroring is destructive, difficult on your physiology, or just plain depressing. Imagine the time when you must achieve agreement with an individual who chain smokes and you do not smoke at all. How can you match them and develop rapport? This exercise will teach you a refinement in the matching scheme and teach you how to gain rapport without getting lung cancer.

Exercise #13

1. Person A will talk to B about anything of mutual interest.

2. Mirror posture; as A is talking, B will take up the body posture of A.

3. Mirror breathing; as A is speaking, B will mirror A's breathing pattern.

4. Mirror predicates; as A is speaking, B will match predicates with A. Match type, order and frequency of predicate.

5. Cross-over mirroring; choose predicates, breathing or body movement and mirror but in a different system. For example, if you choose to cross-over mirror A's breathing, you might tap your foot in rhythm to A's inhaling and exhaling.

6. Work for five minutes on each category and rotate.

7. Further work; consider mirroring the following:

> a) hand gestures
> b) head gestures
> c) placement of body parts
> d) weight shifts
> e) body movements through space
> f) facial movements and expressions
> g muscle tension
> h) eye accessing cues
> i) voice tone, tempo, pitch and volume
> j) tempo of body movements

Body Sculpting

Purpose

To discover a new, non-English language to communicate with.

Explanation

What does it take to make yourself understood? How do you know when you have been understood? In our everyday life, we think we know what others are thinking and we prove it when we say, "You know . . ." and they say, "Yes." What really happens is that we know what we think they meant when they describe something, but in fact, we have no way of being sure that what we have in mind is the same thing they have in mind. This exercise explores a little of what it takes to make yourself understood.

Exercise #14

1. Person A is seated in a pose that he can maintain for about eight minutes. It will be easier for A if he fixes his eyes on some object in the environment. When the eyes are fixed, so is the physiology.

2. C is seated in front of A and must describe A's pose to B. B cannot see A. An easy way for you to arrange yourselves is around a door way. See the diagram below.

3. The trick is that C may not speak or even move any part of his body except his head. B cannot ask any questions but must get all his information about A by C's non-English, non-motioned communication.

4. Rotate and do this exercise again but this time do it by touch instead of sound. Use your sense of touch to describe the pose but do not touch the body part being described or moved. Use pressure, movement, speed, etc. to communicate the pose.

Enter Seating Diagram

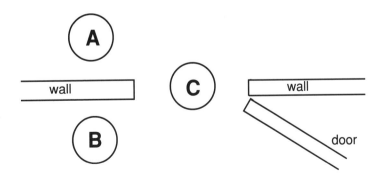

Matching and Mismatching

Purpose

To demonstrate the effects on rapport when matching or mis-matching predicates and posture.

Explanation

There are people in your life with whom you immediately gain rapport. It is as if you knew them all your life, when in fact you may have only just met. There are others with whom you must find a way to co-exist. You might know them very well through work or some other forced situation, and yet it is very difficult even to get along. What causes each of these situations? What is it about each type of person that makes them instantly loved or repulsed? This exercise will teach you more about body language than you ever thought possible. It is about how rapport happens.

Exercise #15

1. Person A will speak to B about any topic of interest.

2. Divide the exercise into four parts and run for five minutes in each part;

> a) B matches A's posture and predicates;
> b) B matches A's posture but mismatches predicates;
> c) B matches A's predicates but mismatches posture;
> d) B mismatches A's posture and predicates.

3. Stretch. Match and mismatch tone, tempo and tonality as B responds to A.

Relevancy Challenge

Purpose

To teach the ability to defend your outcome without sacrificing rapport.

Explanation

As you wend your way through life, you will probably accumulate goals along the way. These goals are very important to you but may not be important to anyone else. In fact, your goals may conflict with the goals of others in your environment. The trick is that you must live in the world and be able to co-exist with all the other people you come in contact with. How can you achieve your goals while maintaining rapport with those around you? This exercise will give you some practice at making up a goal, getting to that goal, and still having a few friends left at the end of it all.

Exercise #16

1. In groups of three, A and B decide on a topic A knows something about.

2. A and C will agree on a signal system and keep it a secret from B. It might be a specific type of cough or a twitch of a finger or some other easily identified signal.

3. B will ask A specific questions directed towards filling in his knowledge of A's topic. B's outcome will be to gain in-depth knowledge about A's topic. B should be very specific about the topic he chooses.

4. As the questions and answers proceed, C will signal to A to become irrelevant.

5. B's job is to notice the shift to irrelevance and to bring A back on track. A whack on the side of the head will work fine, but B's job is to keep rapport and achieve his outcome of gaining specific knowledge.

6. Stretch. Use the same set up, but this time B brings A back on track without using words. B can shift posture, change eye accessing cues, etc. A very simple yet powerful way to communicate displeasure is to noticeably shift from rapt attentiveness to disinterest. Suddenly look at your watch and move in your chair. This is stuff you have been using all your life. Now you begin to understand how and why it works.

7. Go for subtlety.

Six Step Reframing

Purpose

To change old behavior and substitute new behavior.

Explanation

This is a powerful exercise for developing rapport with yourself or for helping a friend develop new choices. It is surprising how little attention we pay to ourselves and to our internal processes. This exercise will teach the development of an internal signal system so that you can discover why you do the things you do - especially those things which you know are destructive. Use this process as a behavior generator. In this exercise you will develop the ability to replace old, destructive or counter-productive behavior with new, useful behavior. This technique can be used with any problem, alone or in a group. It is one of the most useful of all the NLP techniques for bringing about personal evolution.

Exercise #17

1. Identify the pattern (X) to be changed. "I want to stop 'X'ing but I can't" or "I want to Y, but X stops me."

2. Establish communication with the part responsible for the pattern.

> a) Ask, "Will the part of me that makes me X communicate with me in consciousness now?" Pay attention to any feelings, images, or sounds that occur in response to asking that question internally. This is your signal.
> b) Once a signal is noticed, establish the "yes/no" meaning of the signal. Have it increase in brightness, volume or intensity for "yes" and decrease for "no."

3. Separate the behavior, pattern X, from the positive intention of the part that is responsible for X. The unwanted behavior is only a way to achieve some positive outcome.

> a) Ask the part that runs X, "Would you be willing to let me know in consciousness what you are trying to do for me by pattern X?"
> b) If you get a "yes" response, ask the part to go ahead and communicate its intention. If you get a "no," proceed with unconscious reframing, presupposing positive intention.

c) Ask, "Is that intention acceptable to conscious-ness? Do you want to have a part of you that fulfills that function?"

d) Ask the part that runs X, "If there were ways to accomplish your positive function that would work as well as, or better than X, would you be willing to try them out?"

4. Access a creative part and generate new behaviors to accomplish the positive function.

a) Access experiences of creativity and anchor them, or ask, "Are you aware of a creative part of yourself?"

b) Have the part that runs X communicate its positive function to the creative part, allow the creative part to generate more choices to accomplish that function, and have the part that used to run X select three choices that are at least as good or better than X. Have it give a "yes" signal each time it selects such an alternative.

5. Ask the part, "Are you willing to take responsibility for using the three new alternatives in the appropriate context?" This provides a future pace. In addition, you can ask the part at the unconscious level to identify the sensory cues that will trigger the new choices and to experience fully what it is like to have those sensory cues effortlessly and automatically bring on one of the new choices.

6. Ecology check. Ask, "Is there any part of me that objects to any of the three new alternatives?" If there is a "yes" response, recycle to step #2 above and find out other choices.

Content Reframe, Context Reframe

Purpose

To teach flexibility of thinking and speech. This exercise offers a useful way to change perceptions.

Explanation

This is a good mental gymnastics exercise. It becomes exciting to keep content and context straight in your mind as you proceed. The usefulness of this exercise is to teach instant creativity. How many positive things can you say about a seemingly negative occurrence or circumstance? This is the ultimate lesson on how to become one of the positive people.

Exercise #18

1. Two people are involved in a conversation. Person A is very resourceful, while B has a problem.

2. B states his problem. A's job is to reframe the problem in three different ways. A can do a context reframe or a content reframe:

> a) Content Reframing is when you keep the event or content the same but find a new meaning for the behavior. For example: The problem is, "smoking is a horrible habit and I wish I could stop."The reframe: "For many people, smoking is a way of rewarding themselves."
> b) Context Reframe is where the meaning of the behavior does not change but an appropriate place is found where the behavior makes sense. For example: the problem might be, "I hate it when I scream at my kids. I never want to do it again." The reframe can be: "Think how important it is for you to be able to scream at your kids. Just the other day I saw Johnny nearly wander into the traffic on your street . . .".

3. Stretch by doing three content or three context exercises. Identify each type as you go.

Reframing A System

Purpose

To interrupt and change a stimulus-response loop.

Explanation

This is similar to the six step reframing exercise we went through earlier, but in this case, the reframe is applied to a system. In this exercise, a system means any group of players: several workers in your office, several corporations on Wall Street, several members in your household, etc. This exercise is especially useful in any interpersonal conflict and is a technique used by many negotiators in getting to agreement.

Exercise #19

1. Identify a two participant loop. This can be between two parts of yourself or between two people. Participant X communicates to the other participant Y, creating a negative response when a different response was intended.

2. Ask the responding participant:

> a) "Are these feelings (Y) familiar?"
> b) "What is the message you get when he does X?"

3. Ask the stimulus participant:

> a) "Is that (Y) what you intended by doing X?"
> b) "What did you intend?"

4. Ask the stimulus participant, "Are you committed to getting your intended message across?"

5. Find a way to make the message received the same as the message intended.

> a) Find the resources in the experience of the stimulus participant. "Have you ever gotten the response you wanted? What did you do then?" Have them get a complete visual, auditory and kinesthetic representation and, when satisfied, step into it.

b) Find the resources in the experience of the recipient. "What behavior would work to elicit the response in you?" Coach the stimulus participant until he duplicates the behavior.

c) Select a model or pretend that you know how to get that response. Develop a full representation. Check visual, auditory and kinesthetic systems for completeness, and handle any objections, redesigning as necessary.

6. Have the stimulus participant try out the new behavior to find out if it works satisfactorily. Check with the recipient.

7. Future pace.

Agreement Frame

Purpose

To achieve agreement between two people.

Explanation

This exercise allows practice for all future negotiators and conflict resolution experts. Of course, it is really useful for everyone because we are all in conflict all of the time. For example, I want to visit with my son, but he wants to watch cartoons. There is no end to the applications of the successful practice of this exercise.

Exercise #20

1. Person A and B have a difference of opinion about something.

2. Meta-Person C asks A and B for a specific description of their outcome. C restates their outcome to insure accuracy and as a pace.

3. C asks both A and B what their specific outcome will do for them and again restates it.

4. Find a common outcome such that when C states it, both A and B will agree it is what they want. This requires chunking up to the lowest level at which their goals are the same.

5. Once agreement has been achieved, chunk back down in small steps to the lowest possible level of specificity while keeping agreement.

6. Show both A and B how they want the same thing at several levels and ask their cooperation in achieving their mutual goals.

Kinesthetic Advisor

Purpose

To use personal resources which are not normally available to help yourself.

Explanation

This exercise will facilitate an intra-personal rapport. Many folks find it hard to trust themselves or even to communicate with their inner parts. One of the underlying assumptions of NLP is that our internal parts have a positive intent. Since making decisions is tough enough as it is, why not tap into another source of wisdom? This exercise gives you the ability to access this inner wealth of knowledge.

Exercise #21

1. A and B will work at helping A get in touch with an inner advisor.

2. A sits comfortably in a chair and thinks of a less than ideal situation with which she needs help. B helps talk A into this state which they want to work on. As A begins to sink into this less than fully resourceful state, B takes A's hand and lifts her out of the chair. B is doing two things here; (a) he is kinesthetically anchoring the problem state with a touch on the hand, and (b) he is causing a change in A's state. When you change the physiology, you change the state.

3. B instructs A to stand behind the chair she was sitting in. Have the real A touch the imaginary body of herself as she sits in the chair. B will increase this kinesthetic dissassociation by talking A around A's imaginary head and shoulders: "feel your hair," "How do your ears feel to the touch?", "Notice your skin temperature on your cheeks," etc. Develop a complete disassociation.

4. Once A is fully kinesthetically dissassociated, ask the standing A what resources she has that would be of use to the sitting A. As the standing A sorts through and develops the resources, anchor by touching her hand in the same way you used to pull her off the chair. Stack anchors in this way.

5. Once the standing A is satisfied that she has the resources she needs, take her hand (triggering the anchor in the process) and lead her back to the chair. As A begins to sit, say "I want you both to join and solve your problems in new ways."

6. If you notice A falling back into the physiology of the problem state, trigger the anchor again. Repeat until you see A sitting in the chair in a resourceful state.

Internal Conflict Manager

Purpose

To assist in conflict resolution when parts of the same person refuse to get along.

Explanation

Remember the last time you had difficulty making a big decision? It was difficult partly because so much was at stake but also because it seemed that your objectives were at odds with each other. One part of you wanted to say yes and one part wanted to say no. This experience is common to all of us, but there is a way to resolve these internal conflicts. The usefulness of this exercise will be apparent the next time you have difficulty deciding what to do.

Exercise #22

1. Use three identical chairs. Sit on the center chair and place one chair on each side of you. Identify and clearly separate the parts which are in disagreement. Once the two conflicting parts are identified, place each one in a chair. Get a full visual, kinesthetic and auditory representation of each part in their separate chairs.

2. Find out what each part wants in order for it to feel fulfilled. Find out why each part is in conflict with the other.

3. Chunk up to the lowest possible level where both agree on a shared outcome. If the parts are in serious conflict, you may have to chunk all the way up to the survival of the person.

4. Negotiate: what does each part want from the other? What trades must be made? What contracts entered into for each to be satisfied?

5. Get each part to agree to signal the other when something is needed, such as more time, more space, permission, appreciation, attention, affection, etc.

6. Integrate; ask each part if it is willing to integrate with the other in order to more efficiently approach the problem and communicate about it. If the answer is yes, integrate the two parts together. If no, keep the parts separate.

7. Reintegrate; bring both parts back into your body physically. These two conflicting parts may have been integrated into one cooperative whole or they may continue to be two separate entities, but it is important to bring the parts back into yourself. Some rather serious confusion results from failure to reintegrate. Don't leave home without your parts.

Circle of Excellence

Purpose

To create a state of confidence.

Explanation

How would you like to have a tremendously powerful ally constantly at your beck and call? Is there ever a time when, going into a situation, you would like to be more capable than you have been in the past? This exercise teaches you how to plan for the future using all the best of your past or the past of someone you know. Research has shown that the subconscious cannot tell the difference between real practice and imagined practice; they both prepare you for an upcoming event for which you want to be at your best. This exercise will show you how to access your best state any time you need it.

Exercise #23

1. Imagine an invisable circle on the floor. Make it three feet in diameter and two feet in front of you.

2. Go inside and recall a time when you were wonderful. Everything went smoothly, you were witty, bright, capable and a great success. If you do not have any personal history of confidence great enough to use in this exercise, you may simply pretend you do have the history and proceed, or you may use any other person's history. You can use a movie hero, a living (or dead) legend, or anyone you admire. The amazing thing about your brain is that it can't tell the difference between "real" history and personal "imagined" history or the history or others. Go ahead, no one will know!

3. Develop a full disassociated visual, auditory and kinesthetic representation of this state. See yourself in the circle being wonderful. Overhear yourself responding wittily. Feel yourself gushing with pride.

4. Move into the circle of excellence. Step into the picture of yourself. Anchor this with a kinesthetic anchor as a resource state so that you may bring it up as required at any time.

Note: this exercise does not create competence. It assumes ability is in place. When ability is not enough and a dose of confidence is required, this exercise works a small miracle. Please be aware of the important difference between confidence and competence!

Circle of Curiosity

Purpose

To teach chaining of anchors and to give the student a choice when he encounters stress.

Explanation

There are people in your life that cause you to go into a less than resourceful state. Perhaps they trigger an old anchor for defeat. They may clash with your preferred representational system so completely that they cause you to go into a nonproductive state. In any case, there is a way to resolve your inability to communicate with these folks. All you need are the tools to unlock the abilities you presently have. Aren't you curious about what these tools are? This exercise teaches the ability to work with any personality type.

Exercise #24

1. The Meta-Observer (Person C) will assist Person A in remembering three separate experiences of curiosity and help him develop them visually, auditorally and kinesthetically, setting an anchor point on the arm. C then directs A to step into an imaginary circle to fully embody each experience. It may be helpful for C to trigger the anchor for A as A steps into the circle.

2. Person C now helps Person A demonstrate the behavior of a person who induces stress in him in a given situation. Person B will practice Person A's representation until it communicates the behavior accurately. C has A break state and sit back down.

3. B now does the behavior for A. C watches A for the moment he begins to enter a stressful condition. He then pulls him out of the chair and out of sight of B. As he does this, he fires both the curiosity anchor and touches A on the shoulder at the same time. He then asks A to step into his circle of curiosity and find the resources needed to handle the situation and makes sure that the resource state is more powerful than the stress situation. C tells A to access this new state as soon as he first encounters the stress. Then he directs A back to his starting point and has B demonstrate the behavior again. C notices A's responses to be sure they are more resourceful.

4. C now arranges a secret signal with B. The signal will instruct B to trigger A's stressful behavior. A and B will now interact benignly. At the signal, B will begin provoking stress in A. It is A's job to trip his own anchor this time and to come out resourceful. If C notices A having difficulty, he may help but only to the extent required to help A in ultimately achieving his own independent resources.

Precision Model: Language Drill

Purpose

Exploring the Meta-model in order to teach a more precise way to speak and think.

Explanation

When we speak with a friend, we often imagine that we understand what each other is thinking. We know the other person fairly well and usually the topic of conversation is familiar, so we act as if we really know what the other person is saying and that we understand them. It is probable that we do understand much of what is said, but there is certainly a lot that goes over our heads. This exercise teaches the ability to identify when you are not getting information even though it seems you are. Dr. Erikson is famous for his fluff sentences. These are the opposite of the Meta-model and are examples of the Milton model. I won't take up the Milton model at this time, but suffice it to say that sentences can be constructed which say absolutely nothing and yet sound very specific and precise. The Meta-model is a way of discovering and correcting incompleteness of the spoken word.

Exercise #25

1. The background:

   The Meta-model is a method of thinking about language. It provides a way to become more precise in our speaking.

   The Meta-model provides five classes of challenges to the casually spoken word:

Violation	Challenge
a) Unspecified nouns "She likes it . . ."	Who, which, what specifically
b) Unspecified verbs "Sue really went . . ."	How, in what way specifically
c) Comparisons "Bill is faster . . ."	more/less than what
d) Universal "Everyone is going . ."	All? None? What would happen if the opposite occurred?
e) Modal operators "I can't possibly . . ."	What makes it necessary? What would happen if we did?

2. The exercises:

   a) Six people are ideal for this exercise. If you have fewer, double up on challenges taken.
   b) Person 1 says a sentence out loud.

Precision Model: Language Drill

As you go around the circle, Persons 2 through 6 will issue challenges to 1's sentence. It is not important that Person 1 respond to the challenges. This exercise is designed to raise your awareness of these meta violations.

c) Person 2 analyzes the sentences for unspecified nouns. If any are found, Person 2 will make the appropriate challenge. If no unspecified nouns are contained within the sentence, Person 2 passes on to Person 3.

d) Person 3 analyzes the sentence to determine if it has any unspecified verbs. If there are any, provide the challenge.

e) Person 4 looks for comparisons and challenges them appropriately when found.

f) Person 5 is looking for universal operators and challenges when found.

g) Person 6 looks for modal operators and challenges accordingly.

h) Rotate one position to the left. Begin with a new sentence and have each person look for a new component under the Meta-model.

Metaphor

Purpose

To learn to talk in meaningful fluff in order to assist others in change.

Explanation

Metaphor is a nifty way to get your point across. It allows you to do therapy without the appearance of therapy and therefore without the resistance often encountered when doing therapy. Telling a metaphor is just like telling a story, except that there is a moral that is useful to the person for whom the metaphor is intended. If you can make up a story, you can tell a metaphor. All you need is a little dash or creativity, a knowledge of the relevant facts, and a clear outcome in mind. The person hearing the story will figure out how the moral is to be applied and what important learning is contained within.

Exercise #26

1. A and B sit comfortably. A has something she needs to work on in her life.

2. B will tell a three to five minute story (a metaphor) from her experience. B does not know what A needs to work on but will mold her story to A's needs anyway. B will do this molding by carefully watching A's unconscious feedback. For example, if A looks up, paint her a verbal picture. B will match predicates, posture, breathing, eye accessing cues and other sensory acuity based feedback as needed to keep rapport and to keep meaningfulness for A.

3. B stays with the story line well enough to be interesting but stays fluffy enough so that A can gain her own learning.

4. When done with the story, A recites the most important points of the story back to B.

5. B has succeeded when: (a) A's most important points are different from what B had in mind, and (b) when A get something meaningful from the story.

New Orleans Flexibility Drill #1

Purpose

To develop flexibility of behavior in internal and external states in order to deal with others more resourcefully.

Explanation

There are people in your life who upset you. Under some circumstances it may be appropriate to let them think they are succeeding when in fact they are not. By separating what is going on inside from what you present to the world outside, you gain time in which you can formulate a response. This is in contrast to an immediate, knee-jerk type of response which many people usually follow. This exercise sounds as if it will induce schizophrenia, and I have to say this procedure feels a little odd when you are doing it, but you gain a strange sense of time and control of events when in this state. You will find the ability to operate in this time-disassociated state useful and this exercise to be a lot of fun.

Exercise #27

1. Person B will describe behavior he finds disturbing in others to A. A will practice behaving in this way in order to elicit a less-than-resourceful state in B. If your group has three participants, Person C will act as Meta and will assist A in perfecting his role as antagonist to B.

2. A will repeat the behavior several times. The object is to really bother B. The more effective A is at provoking B, the better B will become trained.

3. B goes inside and finds the resources he needs in order to deal with people like A. B anchors these resources within himself. If required, B may stack anchors to develop the resource state more fully.

4. A tests B's resourcefulness by attempting to provoke B. B fires his anchors and either succeeds at thwarting A's provocation or succumbs. If B is successful, go to #5. If less than fully successful, go back to #3 and stack more experiences and/or develop the resource state experiences more fully.

5. B will enter into another interaction with A. B will trigger his anchor prior to the encounter and will be at ease internally but will pretend to have the original non-resourceful response externally as exhibited in #1 above. At a prearranged time, B will "snap into" an external state of excellence.

6. During the time when B is exhibiting external incompetence, he is to be planning his response. When he shifts to external competence, he begins his response.

New Orleans Flexibility Drill #2

Purpose

To teach behavioral flexibility.

Explanation

There are behaviors you find repugnant and cannot imagine yourself ever doing. Yet it would be useful to do these behaviors at certain times. I have a friend who says he would never under any circumstances kill an animal. Imagine the time when you are driving down a country road with your family at 60 miles per hour, and a chipmunk springs up onto the road. It is probably better to splat the chipmunk than to endanger your family (maybe better yet to slow down). The point is that there is almost always a time when any behavior you can think of will be appropriate. The concept of requisite variety says that when two systems (people, machines, corporations, etc.) interact, the system with the most flexibility will control or dominate the interaction. If you are ever to exercise any option in your behavioral repertoire, you must be able to generate those patterns. Even though you cannot imagine ever needing that behavior, it is important that you be able to use it. This drill removes mental barriers to flexibility by teaching the ability to perform those behaviors.

Exercise #28

1. In groups of three, A chooses behavior X that is uncomfortable for him but would be useful at times. Describe this behavior and the context in which you would like to use it to B.

2. B will help A find and access the resources he needs to do X.

3. B provides A's context in order to facilitate A's demon-stration of X.

4. B helps A maintain resourcefulness. A practices his ability to access the resources he needs to do behavior X.

5. Test demonstration with B: A starts out unresourceful and as the scene proceeds, the Meta-Observer, C, will signal A to access his resources. Success is achieved when A can access the behavior he wants when he wants it.

Developing Non-Dominant Systems

Purpose

To teach the development of a representational system that you think you are not using or would like to enhance beyond your present limited use.

Explanation

Everyone has a preferred representational system. The preference may be weak or strong, but there is always a hierarchy of systems. Your other two systems are waiting to be developed. By practicing a little, you can develop greater awareness of your non-dominant representational systems. This will allow you more flexibility in your behavior and more flexibility in your internal processes. It is also a lot of fun to see movies in your head for the first time or to have a chat with yourself when that concept had never occurred to you before. Pushing the limits of your own human possibilities is an exciting and rewarding way to spend the next couple of years. These skills also assist in building rapport as they allow you to match systems with your partner.

Exercise #29

1. Development of Visualization Ability

   If you are auditory:

   a) Sit comfortably and go inside.
   b) Remember a pleasant experience and begin by talking to yourself about it. As you develop this memory, add some of the non-word sounds that went with the experience. If you were at the beach, listen to the sound of the waves superimposed onto your conversation. Add other background sounds.
   c) As you hear the sounds, imagine what the source of those sounds might look like. For waves, see a picture of waves you have seen before. If the imagined picture is hard to get, try it as a snapshot versus a movie. Play with doing it in color or black and white. Put the picture on a movie screen or in a picture frame. Add detail or make the picture include only the source of the sounds.
   Experiment with adding or subtracting visual elements.There is a combination which will make it easier for you to get a picture.
   d) Once you have the start of a picture, let it develop by adding more elements.
   e) Experiment by adding feelings which might be associated with your sounds and sights. You can develop a full visual, auditory and kinesthetic representation with practice.

If you are Kinesthetic:

a) Sit comfortably and go inside.
b) Remember a pleasant experience and begin to feel it.
c) As you are deepening the feelings associated with the experience, notice the subtle changes in your physiology and continue to deepen your awareness of the experience.
d) When you reach a certain point in your comfort, look for any snatches of color or movement that go along with the feelings. Listen for any sounds that go with your feelings.
e) Notice which feelings specifically cause you to have small flashes of pictures. Go to these feelings and stay there awhile. Develop any bit of a picture. If it is a color, intensify it. If it is a shape, sharpen it. If it is movement, slow it down until you can clearly see what is moving.
f) Continue playing with these elements until you get more building blocks with which you can build a full picture.

The general pattern is here is called synesthesia. This is a jumping from one system which is caused by operation in another. Use your strength in one main system to develop a memory. Transfer to your next strongest system to further develop your representation of the experience. Finally, use the resources of your two stronger representational systems to bring in the elements of your weakest system. You can use this pattern to develop any weak system starting from any stronger pattern. I will leave the specifics of getting to kinesthetic representations from the visual, and so on, to your abilities to generalize the above.

Double Disassoci-
ation Phobia Cure

Purpose

To develop a cure for what scares you.

Explanation

This is an exercise and, as such, is useful for learning NLP technology. But this is also a real live therapeutic technique and is tremendously powerful. This piece is used to eliminate phobias in your willing clients and in yourself and also to recognize that feelings are changeable.

Exercise #30

1. Find a phobia. Don't experience it, just find it.

2. Imagine you are in a movie theater. Up on the screen is a black and white snapshot in which you see yourself in a situation just before you have the phobic response.

3. Float out of your body up to the projection booth of the theater where you can watch yourself watching yourself. From this position you'll be able to see yourself sitting in the middle of the theater and also in the still picture on the screen.

4. Turn the snapshot on the screen into a black and white movie; watch it from the beginning to just beyond the end of the unpleasant experience. When you get to the end, stop it and jump inside the picture. Run it backwards but this time in color.

5. Test yourself to see if the phobic response is changed.

6. This phobia cure can be done effectively in many ways. The key is to make sure the client feels safe. Safety is achieved in two ways; first, be sure there is multiple disassociation. This literally puts space between the client and what they are afraid of. Secondly, use submodality changes to de-energize the emotional content of the phobia. It is very difficult to keep a strong phobic response when you change the movie; make it move in reverse, black and white from color, slow it down or speed it up, make it silent and small in size. Make as few changes as required to get results and as many as you must to drain off the emotional energy.

Confusion into Clarity Doubt into Certainty

Purpose

To create understanding where confusion used to be. To use the same procedure on doubt and certainty.

Explanation

Have you ever been in a situation where you thought you had all the information you needed to make a decision but were still confused or uncertain about what to do? Confusion about a subject may be due to a lack of specific information or it may be because of the way you have represented the situation to yourself internally. We have seen how easy (and fun) it is to change these internal representations. This exercise teaches representational change work for your benefit and for those around you who need to be more certain and less confused.

Exercise #31

1. Work in groups of two, A and B.

2. Person A will think of (a) something he is confused about, and (b) something similar he understands. He is not allowed to tell Person B about the content.

3. B will ask A, "How are these two experiences different?" It is not important how they are the same. Go for the differences.

4. When you have at least two differences, ask A to change confusion to be the same as understanding. Modify the picture, sounds or feelings to make both conditions the same.

5. Test what you've done by asking if the other person understands what was previously confusion. If he does, you're done. If he doesn't, back up to Step #2 and find some more differences. Keep going until he understands or has identified specifically what information he is missing which prevents full understanding. This techniques provides one of two valuable outcomes; it will create understanding or it will show what is necessary for understanding to happen. However, it will not grant you a Ph.D. in nuclear physics.

Note: This comparison and change work also succeeds with doubt and certainty. Go through the procedure again, comparing and then modifying those pictures, sounds or feelings of doubt and certainty.

The Swish Pattern

Purpose

The Swish is a very generative pattern that can be used for just about anything. It is a technique for creating new behavior.

Explanation

Have you ever wished you could quit overtipping waitresses when you go out to eat? It is a common problem I know. Or how about that persistent urge to eat ice cream even though you are totally full and thirty pounds overweight? Changing behavior patterns is not easy when your main ally is willpower. Many patterns have been in place for a lifetime, and unless they are really easy things that you don't care much about anyway, changing them requires more willpower than it is worth. The Swish is a pattern changer par excellence. You can change any pattern that you can identify. This is one of the most versatile and powerful of all the NLP techniques for personal change work.

Exercise #32

1. In groups of two, one person will assist the other in changing an unwanted behavior.

2. Person A will help B in identifying the context. First identify what pattern B wants to change. Where or when would he like to behave or respond differently than he does now? You can pick something like nail biting or something like getting angry at your boss.

3. Help B identify the cue picture. What do you actually see in that situation just before you start doing the behavior you don't like? If you have trouble getting this picture, try doing it and notice what you see. Since this is the cue for a response you don't like, there should be at least some unpleasantness associated with this picture. The more unpleasant this is, the better it will work.

4. Create the outcome picture. Create a second image of how you would see yourself differently if you had already accomplished the desired change. Adjust this image until you have one that is really attractive to you, one that draws you strongly.

5. Swish: Swish by seeing that cue picture, big and bright up on a movie screen. Start out by being in the picture while doing the old behavior and have it fill the screen. Place a small dim snapshot of your new behavior in a corner of the movie screen. Let the snapshot swish up from the corner. As it fills the screen, make it a color movie of your desired behavior. The critical element of the swish is that you start out in the picture of the unwanted behavior and swish to a position outside the new behavior. This is called going from the associated representation to the disassociated. You might accomplish this by imagining yourself jumping into the audience of the movie theater and watching over your shoulder as you do the new behavior.

6. Repeat; do this five times. Be sure to open your eyes or blank the screen between swishes.

7. Test. Ask yourself to "picture the first image." If this is difficult to do, the swish has been effective. You will find the first picture will fade into the second desired picture.

Experience vs. Hallucination

Purpose

To improve your skills as an observer and to demonstrate that you rarely know what anyone else is really thinking or experiencing.

Explanation

I remember seeing a Psychology 1 experiment where a photograph of a smiling person was shown to the members of the class and the subject of the experiment was to guess what emotions and circumstances the person in the photograph was experiencing. We went around the class and each person gave what seemed a very plausible explanation of why this person was smiling. Afterwards, the whole photo was shown and we could see the context of what was really going on. It turned out that a flood had occurred in this town and all the buildings had been destroyed. The person in the photo was smiling because he saw a dog that had been saved by climbing up onto a phone pole. This is a pretty long winded introduction to the idea that we really never know what is going on inside another person's mind, because we can never really know the full context of their thoughts. This point is brought home very nicely in the following exercise.

Exercise #33

1. Observation:

a) In groups of 2 or 3, Person B's job is detection. Person A will practice experiencing different kinds of states. C's job is to help B observe accurately and to keep things moving along.

b) A will select three different experiences that he had which were very intense. They can be from any part of his life but should be distinct from each other. He should not make any comments about them, but simply number them in his head.

c) A will join hands with B. B will calibrate to A's "neutral state." This is how A is in the here and now. Anything else is a product of the remembered experience. A will then announce "one" and will go inside and recreate experience #1. It is important that A's experience be as full as possible. Intensify the pictures, sounds, and feelings until the experience seems as if it is just happening for the first time. It is also imperative that the experience as remembered by A is in the associated state. See what you would have seen through your own eyes if you were there. Do not look at yourself doing it.

Experience vs. Hallucination

> d) Once B has noticed state "one," A will do a break
> state and come back to neutral. A will then an-
> nounce "two," grasp B's hand and produce a full
> internal representation of two. Again, B will observe
> this expression of A's experience.
> e) Break state, then repeat for a third time with
> "three."
> f) Notice the profound changes A has gone through.

2. Calibration:

> a) Do the exact same sequence of experience
> generation but this time B will describe the observed
> changes in A out loud to C.
> b) The observations must be sensory based de
> criptions: "The corners of her eyes turn up slightly
> and her cheeks are rising. Her breathing is shallow
> and rapid." Happy or worried are judgements and
> as such as not sensory based and are not allowed.

3. Guessing:

> a) This time A will go into one of the experiences
> without identifying it. B will guess which experience
> A has chosen.
> b) A will continue running through the experiences in
> any order until B can correctly identify which experi-
> ence A is producing.

4. Hallucination:

> a) This time A goes into one of the experiences and
> B guesses (hallucinates) about the content of the
> experience.
> b) Enjoy this. All the experiences up to now have
> been sensory based. This is the first time you have
> permission to add your own map of reality to what
> you see.

5. Recycle with new group members.

I Trust Myself

by Tarn Singh and Pascal Gambardella*

Purpose

To teach self trust and experience separating self from behavior.

Explanation

This exercise was introduced to my practitioner class by Susan Marcus. She put us in a trance and we proceeded with what follows. My personal experience was a much fuller sense of the different parts of myself and to appreciate them much more. The folks in my group found this to be a very profound experience.

* Reprinted with permission from The VAK International Newsletter, Palo Alto, CA.

Exercise #34

1. This exercise is best done when two people, a Programmer and a Subject, are involved. If you want to work alone, I suggest you use a tape recorder. Speak the script onto a tape while working as the Programmer. Play the tape back while you listen and respond as the Subject.

2. Programmer: have the Subject think of a recent experience in which she can say, "I trusted myself." In making this statement, the Subject speaks of two entities, the "I" and the "myself" and their relationship, one of trusting. Have the Subject answer the questions below.

Note: the questions are a suggested list. Tailor the questions to the individual and context. Other entities may appear while the Subject answers the questions for the "I" and "myself." If so, use these questions to discover the qualities of those entities as well.

3. Describe the "I." Where is the "I" located? What are its visual, auditory or kinesthetic qualities? Is it primarily visual, auditory or kinesthetic? Is it primarily oriented toward the past, present or future?How is the "I" responsible toward the "myself"? How is it responsible for (a) how you perceive yourself, (b) how you perceive others, and (c) how you make decisions? Is the "I" trustworthy? What makes it so?

4. Describe the "myself." Where is the "I" located? What are its visual, auditory or kinesthetic qualities? Is it primarily visual, auditory or kinesthetic? Is it primarily oriented toward the past, present or future?How is the "I" responsible toward the "myself"? How is it responsible for (a) how you perceive yourself, (b) how you perceive others, and (c) how you make decisions? Is the "I" trustworthy? What makes it so?

5. Which part (the "I" or the "myself") is primarily responsible for whether you fail or accept feedback? What is their relationship in each case? Which one generates choices for your behavior in the present? In the future?

I Trust Myself

Which one generates and maintains the concept of who you would like to be?

Which one is more trustworthy? Why?

If you could have only one part, which would it be?

Is there anything that either part would like to say to the other?

Note: This exercise can be generalized to other parts of the "I"-"myself" whole. Consider for example; "I love myself," or "I 'X' myself."

Change Personal History

Purpose

To go back in time and change the impact of an event so that you can live happily ever after. A way to change the end of the story.

Explanation

Some people have phobias. A phobia is an intensely fearful response to something today as a result of something which happened some time ago. A phobia is an extreme example of history that needs changing. This exercise teaches a technique for changing less extreme memories. We all have past performances which limit us. ("If I had only said . . ." or "If I had only done . . ., etc.) The techniques of this exercise allow you the opportunity to turn back the hands of time and rewrite the script. You really can change the effects of your mistakes within your own life. This is a very useful way to erase the burden of past mistakes and prepare for a better future reality.

Exercise #35

1. B anchors a base state in A. This is the here-and-now anchor.

2. A develops a full visual, auditory and kinesthetic representation of a past performance of which she wants to change the effects. We will call this behavior "X". B anchors this state.

3. B coaches A back to the first time A can remember doing X. Develop this memory fully in all three representational systems and stack onto the same anchor that X is on now.

4. Bring A back to here-and-now using the base state anchor.

5. Create a resource state in A. Do a full system representation and anchor all the responses that A has now that she might not have had when X first began. We will call the resource anchor "Y".

6. Collapse anchors X and Y. This is most easily done when both anchors are kinesthetic. The collapse will work just as well when the anchors are auditory or visual, but you might find in inconvenient to hum or wave your hands for several minutes at a time.

7. Hold both X and Y anchors until they are fully integrated.

8. Now ask A to return to her first memory of X. Go back to just before she did X. Ask her to replay the experience but have her signal to you when she gets to the decision point, the place just before she X's. When she signals, trigger her resource anchor. Instruct her to "continue replaying the experience but with the new happy ending" (resources).

9. Now go back to the beginning and replay the entire experience without the anchor. If the history has been successfully changed, the new behavior will be what is replayed. If the old behavior is still present, recycle to #5 above.

Strategies

Purpose

To elicit a strategy from someone you wish to model. To learn how to be a "behavioral thief."

Explanation

Every field has experts. There are always one or more individuals who do what they do better than all the rest. Why? What is their secret? NLP offers you the ability to observe in sensory specific detail what someone is doing and to break it down into smaller pieces which can be modeled. In this exercise, you will learn about strategies. How do these exemplary individuals motivate themselves? How do they achieve such success and how can you do it too? There is a method to this madness. There is a series of reproducible steps that these experts go through each time they perform. Using NLP skills learned in earlier exercises, you are now ready to become a behavioral thief.

Exercise #36

1. A has a behavior, "X", that B wants to model.

2. B asks A to pretend he is going to do X.

3. As A goes through the imagined experience of doing X, B notices and records everything he sees in sequential order, such as:

    a) physiology
    b) eye accessing cues
    c) breathing
    d) body movements
    e) statements A is making about content.

4. Bring A back to the present.

5. B now does what A just did (model predicates, physiology, breathing, etc.). Fully install all of A's behaviors. Any deficiencies in B's target state can be noticed and corrected if you have a Meta-Observer in your group.

6. Test: As B fully develops the target state, does A follow along? If A does, B is probably very close to a full and true model of X. As you test, be sure A is not recreating the state internally but is developing the state because of B's interaction externally with him.

7. Go forth and X.

New Behavior Generator

Purpose

To create new behavioral choices in future situations and to try them out ahead of time.

Explanation

Surprise is wonderful on your birthday but not always so wonderful in real life where being unprepared can cost dearly. It is difficult to anticipate every possible situation and prepare for them. However, when you know you are likely to enter into an encounter and that you don't have the strengths you need for this particular situation, the behavior generator will assist you in developing the needed skills ahead of time. Using this technique, you can try out a variety of plausible scenarios and add to or subtract from them as necessary. In this way, when the real situation occurs, you will have practiced the same thing before. Everything is easier the second time around.

Exercise #37

1. B helps A to determine a situation in the future in which A would like to have more behavioral choices and resources. A is to think of this situation but not experience it.

2. B assists A in choosing three alternative behavioral choices for the next time A is faced with this situation or event. A will develop a full visual, kinesthetic and auditory representation of each of these three behavioral alternatives. Anchor each of the three choices to a physical location on the floor in front of A. "I want you to place the resources and the choice to use them over there. See, hear and feel yourself using these resources over there."

3. After A has completely developed these alternatives, ask her which choice would be most appropriate in dealing with this future event. After A has chosen one of the three, walk her up next to but not into the location where that resource was anchored. Have her play a movie of her future event in her head. As she approaches the point in the movie where she must decide how to act, move her into that first resource state and experience the future event with the resource chosen. It is important that she enter the spot anchored at the decision point, because when the real event occurs, you want her to experience choices about her behavior.

4. Do the same with each of the other two choices. Start the movie outside the resource location in a neutral spot. Move into the resource location at the decision point. Let A have the full experience of each of the three possible resources by stepping into each location and running through the future event with each resource. If at any time A discovers that she doesn't like the resources at a particular location, delete that location and anchor a new one with new resources in another spot. Be sure to try out each of the possible choices to be sure they are appropriate and useful.

5. A now has three behavioral alternatives the next time she is faced with the event she has practiced for.

Creating a New Part

Purpose

To generate a new personality part which will result in new choices.

Explanation

This exercise demonstrates the usefulness of multiple personalities! Actually, we are all made up of many parts. We each have an analytical part, a loving part, a part that is responsible for waking us up in the morning, and so on. Occasionally we discover that we are lacking a part. It might be that one day you discover that you would like to be able to tell your boss off but no part exists in you which has the required skills to do so. Or possibly you would like to be able to play the flute, but the part of you responsible for this particular task is missing or greatly underdeveloped. Well, fear not. NLP offers just the ticket for part acquisition.

Exercise #38

1. Identify the desired outcome, the function of the new part, i.e., "I want a part which will achieve Y."

2. Access any historical experience of doing Y. It can be personal history or the history or anyone you know or know of. Step inside each experience and access all aspects of doing Y or parts of Y. Go through each memory in all representational systems.

3. Create a detailed set of images of how you would behave if you were actually demonstrating whatever this part of you is going to have you do to achieve outcome Y:

> a) first create a disassociated visual and auditory constructed movie;
> b) when you see a whole sequence that you're satisfied with, step inside the image and go through the whole sequence again from the inside. Feel what it is like to do these behaviors;
> c) if you are not satisfied, go back to #3a and change the movie. Do this until you are satisfied with that fantasy from the inside as well as from the outside.

4. Ecology check. Ask, "Does any part object to my having a part which will be in charge of making this fantasy a reality?" Make sure you check in all representational systems to find all objecting parts. For each objecting part:

> a) ask that part to intensity the signal for "yes" and decrease for "no";
> b) ask, "What is your function for me? What do you do for me?"
> c) if the function doesn't tell you what the part's objection is, ask, "What specifically is your objection or concern?"
> d) make a complete written list of all the parts that object and their objections.

5. Satisfy all objecting parts;

> a) redefine the part you are creating or take into
> account all the functions and concerns of the
> objecting parts;
> b) go back to Step #3 and make a new or modified
> fantasy that will satisfy the concerns of each part that
> objected;
> c) check with every part to make sure that each one
> is satisfied that this new representation of the new
> part's behavior will not interfere with its function.

6. Ask your unconscious resources to analyze the fantasy and
to pull the essential ingredients from it. Your unconscious is to
use this information to build a part and give it entity. "Get what
you need to know from that fantasy to be able to build a part of
you that can do this exquisitely and easily, and at every moment
that it needs to be done."

7. Test the part to make sure it is there:

> a) go inside and ask;
> b) future pace repeatedly;
> c) behaviorally engage the part to find out if it
> responds appropriately.

Acting As If

Purpose

To teach a new way to access information by creating a contrary-to-fact situation. To learn to pretend.

Explanation

This is probably the easiest of all the exercises in this book. This is because we all have had extensive practice at this technique as kids. Many of us continue to spend many hours a week perfecting these very skills in daily life. The usefulness of this exercise is to develop more behavioral options and to try them out in safe situations before they are required.

Exercise #39

1. Person A will act as if his situation were different with the help of Person B. Person A chooses a topic where he wishes he had a different perspective (perhaps a personal problem or a shortage of creativity).

2. Person B sets the context. He may choose from the list below or make up his own;

> a) person switch; "If you were me, what . . . "
> b) time switch; "Act as if it were six months down the road . . ."
> c) function switch; "If you could change any part of the organization . . ."
> d) information switch; "Let's suppose we knew all about . . . "

3. Person B may find it helpful to anchor a resourceful or creative state prior to starting this part. When ready, B will assist A in pretending he is in a different situation by using phrases such as "Let's suppose that . . .", "If you were to . . .", "Can you act as if . . .", "Pretend that I am . . .", etc.

4. It is A's job to portray the other reality chosen for him as accurately as possible. It is B's job to facilitate this transfer of reality.

Accessing A Drug State

by Ed Reese and Richard Bandler*

Purpose

To teach a powerful process for reaccessing a drug state quickly and fully.

Explanation

This exercise is for those who have enjoyed the use of recreational drugs in the past but for one reason or another choose not to use drugs now. Another reason to learn this technique is that when it is generalized to other experiences it allows you to recreate them, too. For instance, it is a lot more fun to relive a bowl of Haagen-Daz ice cream than to watch late night reruns of *Father Knows Best.* Anyway, use this to enjoy a bowl of your favorite ice cream and skip the calories. Use it instead of dangerous and expensive drugs. Use it any time you want to reexperience what you've been missing.

* Reprinted with permission from The VAK International Newsletter, Palo Alto, CA.

Exercise #40

1. Use a memory of a pleasant drug experience.

2. Identify and make a list of a minimum of five stages in the kinesthetic system which occur as the drug takes effect and you enter the drug state. Notice the very first sensation you have as a part of this state, and take the time to identify the specific qualities of the feeling, exactly where it begins, and what small changes occur as the state progresses. To some extent, the chunking of the kinesthetic changes into five or more stages is arbitrary; what is important is to notice the kinesthetic sensations and sequence in great detail so that you can recreate the experience (and the resulting drug state) at will. If you think, "First, my head feels warm," you can ask, "Where in my head does the warmth first begin? And what happens next?" in order to get a more detailed sequence.

2. Go through the kinesthetic sequence again, identifying and listing the visual or auditory submodalities which change with each of the kinesthetic stages you listed previously.

3. Try adjusting individual submodalities, or the sequence of changes to find out how you can intensify or improve the drug state. How can you make the recreated experience even better than the original one?

Pattern Interruption

Purpose

To teach a useful technique for changing the state of someone you are working with.

Explanation

Pattern interruption is a useful skill to have. Consider the times you have been with someone who has just received some bad news and they begin to slip into depression. Or the time you were with a two year old and he threw a temper tantrum. Pattern interruption is akin to breaking rapport but without going that far.

Exercise #41

1. In groups of three, A and B will talk about any topic of mutual interest. Out of A's sight, C will signal to B to interrupt A's pattern.

2. When B gets the signal, he will do something to interrupt A's pattern. An obvious method to interrupt someone's pattern is to whack them on the side of the head. Be subtle. Do the interruption without breaking rapport.

3. Practice several times. Stretch for a technique that will get A to pause but not to lose their train of thought completely.

4. Experiment with interruptions in each of the representational systems. Try different sounds, sights and touches.

Incongruence Instead of Drugs

Purpose

To teach behavioral flexibility and to experience first-hand this powerful pattern interrupt. To teach the ability to discern when people you interact with daily are not fully congruent.

Explanation

This is a refinement of an exercise we did earlier; Pattern Interruption. This is also useful as a fun parlor game. The value of the exercise is that it teaches a sensitivity to whether the person you think you are talking to is really with you or not.

Exercise #42

1. Two people will interact in a normal, every day way.

2. Person A will keep being normal. Person B will do the following at strategic points throughout the conversation;

> a) agree with A verbally but disagree with his non-verbal expression. He says yes with his mouth but says no with his body.
> b) agree with A non-verbally but disagree verbally. His mouth says no but his body says yes.

Fluff vs. Specificity

Purpose

To learn when to be specific and when to be fluffy in your speech.

Explanation

Until I took my NLP training, I had spent a lifetime trying to be as specific as possible. My formal and informal education taught me that the best way to be understood was to be as explicit as possible and to leave nothing to imagination or interpretation. That technique works pretty well when you are trying to train someone how to flip hamburgers and there is only one best way to flip them. But what about teaching tasks which require creativity? This exercise teaches that the best way to get your message across depends on who is listening and what the message is.

Exercise #43

1. Work in groups of three; A will tell a story to B.

2. B will repeat the story to C. B is to stay as close to the original story line as possible but is to use different words than A used. B will stay as specific in his descriptions as possible.

3. C will repeat the story back to A, staying as close to the story line as possible, using different words, but this time making the words as fluffy as possible.

For example:

> A: "I went up a green hillside. It was very steep and I nearly slipped on the moist spring grass."

> B: "I walked on the side of a green foothill. As I walked, I almost slipped because the grass was moist. It was spring time."

> C: "I was outdoors walking uphill. It was a pleasant time of year. As I was walking, I nearly had an accident."

4. When it is your turn to be A, notice your reaction to each story as it is told.

Traveling Story

Purpose

To teach the ability to be sensory aware on many levels at once.

Explanation

This exercise is very fun and can be used at your next family reunion or baby shower. It is also instructive, of course. The lesson here is sensory acuity and learning to be aware of multiple events happening in different senses. It is very much like learning to play the piano. All of your body parts get into the act and you have to learn to coordinate them.

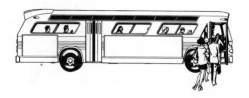

Exercise #44

1. The First Level of Observation:

    a) in groups of four, there will be one person in Meta-Observer fole. The other three people will be seated in a row facing the Meta and will tell a story. The first person is A, the second is B, and the third is C.

    b) Person A starts a story. He speaks a few words, phrases, or sentences as the spirit moves him. When he stops, Person B must pick up the story line and continue on. B must match A's tone, tempo and predicates for fifteen seconds into B's part of the story. B can switch to any other presentation style he chooses after he has matched A.

    c) continue around; A to B, B to C, C to A.

    d) the Meta's job is to insure that the matches are faithful and that the story makes at least some sense. When either of the above conditions is not met, the Meta politely informs the person who missed on the match and trades seats with him.

    e) the new Meta now watches for matches and the story continues around.

2. The Second Level of Observation:

a) Continue around the group with the story but add
a signal. A signal is any observable movement you
choose to make. A might choose as his signal the
touching of his nose. B might make her signal the
placement of both hands a certain way in her lap.
C might make her signal the shuffling of her feet.
b) The signal is started in the same way as the story.
Person A makes his signal. It is A's responsibility to
pace B and C.A can only make his signal as fast as
B and C notice and then do the same signal. If
A gets too far ahead of B and C, the Meta points out
his failure to adequately pace and the Meta and
A trade seats.
c) Once A has made his signal and held it as long as
he likes, he un-does his signal and it becomes
B's turn.
d) The signal system is independent of the story.
They are two separate events which both travel
around the group in the same direction but possibly
at different speeds.
e) If the two followers of the signal fail to notice the
start of the signal even after an appropriate waiting
period has elapsed, or if they fail to match the
proper signal, the Meta catches the non-observant
person and trades seats with him.

3. The Third Level of Observation:

> a) Same set up as above; we will use the story and signal system but this time the signal will not travel around the group in any specific order.
> b) The signal is started and finished. After the finish of the first signal, a second signal is initiated by the same person who just finished his own signal. He now does someone else's signal. Everyone follows in performing this second signal.
> c) When done with this second signal, the person whose signal it was takes a turn and initiates his signal. He then un-does his signal and does someone else's signal and so switches to the next person.
> d) The signal continues to travel in a non-regular path around the group independent of the travel of the story.

Stretch; Make the signal and the story move at different tempos. You can move around the group at different tempos and do the movement itself (raising your hand) to a difference cadence than that of the story.

Therapy By Robot

Purpose

To learn the importance of rapport and with whom to have rapport. You will also learn to do therapy via a robot.

Explanation

This exercise is a chance to integrate all of your previous sensory acuity and rapport building skills. It is surprising to most people to see themselves being portrayed by a robot and many find that their internal sense of what is going on is different than what they see the robot doing externally. It is like listening to yourself on a tape recorder for the first time. This exercise is subtle. The fun you have might mask the important message that nothing can be taken for granted when working with an intermediary. A further lesson comes when you discover that there is always an intermediary between two people. That intermediary is language. In this exercise, you will learn how to overcome a few obstacles and communicate in new and better ways.

Exercise #45

1. You will need four participants for this exercise. One person is the "client" who has a problem. The next player is the "therapist." The client and the therapist will do therapy. The other two folks are the robot and the Meta.

2. The client and the therapist are in opposite corners of the room from each other. They cannot see or hear the interactions between the robot and their counterpart.

3. The robot is the intermediary between the client and the therapist. The robot can be anchored, had rapport with and can be programmed to say certain things. He cannot interpret, create, or originate any behavior. The robot must match the speaker's posture, speech patterns, breathing tone, tempo, and so on. In short, the robot must be a photocopy of what was presented or programmed into him. It is his job to carry the last interaction over to the other partner in the therapist-client exchange. The robot may not in any way add to or subtract from the programming of his last interaction. After all, he is a robot, not a person.

4. The Meta is the traveling companion of the robot. The Meta helps the robot stay resourceful and insures that the robot faithfully relays the messages exactly as they were sent.

5. Do therapy. It can be a "real" problem the client wants work with or it can be made up.

Glossary

ANCHOR: A procedure which allows recall of an experience by either a touch, sound or sight.

> COLLAPSING ANCHORS: When two anchors are triggered simultaneously. The result is the addition oft h e two individual anchors to form a new third anchor.The technique is often used to eliminate an unwanted negative anchor.

> STACKING ANCHORS: Stacking is done to create a stronger anchor. It consists of the recall of several states which are separately anchored in the same anchor. The result is a single anchor that is stronger than any one of the component anchors was separately.

ASSOCIATED STATE: An internal representation or state where you would see, hear and feel the things you would normally experience if you were there physically. Associated simply means in your body in the experience.

DISASSOCIATED STATE: An internal representation or state where you would see, hear and feel the things you would normally experience if you were watching yourself from the outside. It is seeing yourself through another person's eyes. You are outside yourself.

EYE ACCESSING CUES: Movements of the eyes which are symptomatic of the mental processes of retrieving thoughts and experiences stored in the mind.

FLUFF: Spoken words which have an ambiguous meaning. The opposite of concise, specific communication.

FUTURE PACE: A technique done to insure that a learned behavior transfers into the future actions of an individual. It is a mental practice of a new behavior.

INNER PARTS: A term used extensively in NLP to denote the many facets of a personality. This term does not imply a pathological split but rather a recognition that we all have a variety of ways of responding to the same stimulus in the environment.

INTERNAL REPRESENTATION: The internal pictures, sounds and feelings that a person uses when thinking.

OUTCOME: Another name for goal.

PACE: When you match the reality of another person completely. The best pacing is done when physiology and representational systems are matched. The purpose of competent pacing is to establish rapport.

BIBLIOGRAPHY

Bandler, Richard; and Grinder, John. *Frogs Into Princes*. Moab, Utah: Real People Press, 1979.

Laborde, Genie. *Influencing With Integrity*. Palo Alto, CA: Syntony Publishing, 1987.

Lewis, Byron; and Pucelik, Frank. *Magic Demystified*. Portland, OR: Metamorphous Press, 1982.

Kostere, Kim; and and Malatesta, Linda. *Get The Results You Want*. Portland, OR: Metamorphous Press, 1989.

INDEX

Accessing a Drug State   112
Acting As If   110
Agreement Frame   62
Anchor   36
    Criteria   36
    Collapsing   40
    Stacking   36
Associated State   Gloss.
Auditory
    Remembered   12
    Constructed   12
Backtracking   18
Body Sculpting   46
Calibration   92
Challenges   72
Change Personal History   100
Chunking Exercise   20
Circle of Excellence   68
Circle of Curiosity   70
Comparison   72
Confusion into Clarity, Doubt into Certainty   88
Content Reframe   56
Context Reframe   56
Creating a New Part   106
Cross-Over Mirroring   44
Developing Non-Dominant Systems   82
Disassociated State   Gloss.
Double Disassociation Phobia Cure   86
Experience vs. Hallucination   92
Eye Accessing Cues   12
    Watching for   12
Fluff vs. Specificity   118
Future Pace   42
Go Inside, Develop a State of Mind   16
Guess That System   28
How to be Anybody You Want to Be   30
I Trust Myself   96

Incongruence Instead of Drugs	116
Inner Parts	52,106
Internal Conflict Manager	66
Internal Representation	Gloss.
Kinesthetic Advisor	64
Matching	48
Metaphor	76
Mirroring	44
Mismatching	48
Modal Operator	72
New Orleans Flexibility Drill	
#1	78
#2	80
New Behavior Generator	104
Outcome	Gloss.
Picture	90
Pace	Gloss.
Pattern Interruption	114
Precision Model: Language Drill	72
Predicates	
Visual	24
Auditory	24
Kinesthetic	24
Pure	24
Reframing	
a System	58
Six Step	52
Relevancy Challenge	50
Sensory Acuity - Modeling	10
Strategies	102
Submodalities Shift	32
Swish Pattern	90
Tempo	32
Therapy by Robot	124
Traveling Story	120
Unspecified Verbs	72
Violations	72
Visual	
Remembered	12
Construct	12

NOTES

NOTES

NOTES

NOTES

NOTES

NOTES

NOTES

NOTES

NOTES

The Skill Builder Series

The Excellence Principle
Utilizing NeuroLinguistic Programming
Scout Lee, Ed.D.

Basic Techniques, Book I
Linnaea Marvell-Mell

Basic Techniques, Book II
Clifford Wright

Your Balancing Act
Discovering New Life Through Five
Dimensions of Wellness
Carolyn J. Taylor, M.N.C.S.

Advanced Techniques
Phill Boas with Jane Brooks

The Challenge of Excellence
Learning the Ropes of Change
Scout Lee, Ed.D.

Metamorphous Press

Metamorphous Press is a publisher and distributor of books and other media providing resources for personal growth and positive changes. MPI publishes and distributes leading edge ideas that help people strengthen their unique talents and discover that we all create our own realities.

Many of our titles have centered around NeuroLinguistic Programming (NLP). NLP is an exciting, practical and powerful model of human behavior and communication that has been able to connect observable patterns of behavior and communication to the processes that underlie them.

Metamorphous Press provides selections in many subject areas such as communication, health and fitness, education, business and sales, therapy, selections for young persons, and other subjects of general and specific interest. Our products are available in fine bookstores around the world. Among our Distributors for North America are:

Baker & Taylor	The Distributors
Bookpeople	Inland Book Co.
New Leaf Distributors	Moving Books, Inc.
Pacific Pipeline	

For those of you overseas, we are distributed by:

Airlift (UK, Western Europe)
Bewitched Books (Victoria, Australia)

New selections are added regularly and the availability and prices change, so ask for a current catalog or to be put on our mailing list. If you have difficulty finding our products in your favorite store or if you prefer to order by mail, we will be happy to make our books and other products available to you directly. *Your involvement with what we do and your interest is always welcome* - please write to us at:

Metamorphous Press
3249 N.W. 29th Ave.
P.O. Box 10616
Portland, Oregon 97210-0616
(503) 228-4972

NLP Series from
Metamorphous Press

The Skill Builder Series

The Excellence Principle
Scout Lee, Ed.D.
This standard in the field of NLP was originally a set of personal notes and formal thoughts. In its revised form, this workbook is packed with dynamic metaphors, ideas, exercises, and visual aids.
0-943920-71-X paperback $16.95

Basic Techniques, Book I
Linnaea Marvell-Mell
This is the only NLP workbook available for those who wish to refine their NLP skills, people who have read books on the subject or attended seminars but want more. The book comes with a cassette tape. It complements the introductory book, *Magic Demystified*, and reinforces basic NLP skills.
1-55552-016-2 paperback $12.95

Basic Techniques, Book II
Clifford Wright
This workbook provides additional tools to refine skills learned in *Basic Techniques, Book I*. Filled with exercises for individual practice or group work, *Basic Techniques II* provides ongoing skill-building in NLP technology.
1-55552-005-7 paperback $10.95

Your Balancing Act
Carolyn J. Taylor, M.N.C.S.
This NLP text presents systematic exercises and new material for changing the all important beliefs that underlie the conditions of wellness. Health, relationships, creativity and success are just a few aspects addressed.
0-943920-75-2 paperback $12.95

Advanced Techniques
Phill Boas with Jane Brooks
This manual is designed for use by those who have some knowledge of NLP. It is written from the perspective of the trainer/seminar leader and much of the information is intended to help the group leader assist the participants to get maximum benefit from the 50 different exercises.
0-943920-08-6 paperback $9.95

The Challenge of Excellence
Scout Lee, Ed.D.
Scout Lee's book is about utilizing challenge and playfulness to program the human computer for excellence. It has sophisticated information on body language and its connection to the mental process.
1-55552-004-9 paperback $16.95

Positive Change Guides

Get the Results You Want
Kim Kostere/Linda Malatesta
This title provides an explicit model of communication and change which combines the state of the art behavioral technology of Bandler & Grinder with the optimism of humanistic psychology.
1-55552-015-4 paperback $13.95

Fitness Without Stress
Robert M. Rickover
This book explains the Alexander Technique, recognized today to be one of the most sophisticated and powerful methods of personal transformation available. This method can be enjoyed by readers with no previous experience.
0-943920-32-9 cloth $14.95

Magic of NLP Demystified
Byron Lewis & Frank Pucelik
This introductory NLP book is intended to give readers a clear and understandable overview of the subject. It covers the essential elements of NLP and uses illustrations to further explain this behavioral science.
1-55552-017-0 paperback $9.95
0-943920-09-4 cloth $16.95

The Power of Balance
Brian W. Fahey, Ph.D.
The importance of balance in life is the emphasis of Fahey's book. It expands on the original ideas about balancing body structure, known as "Rolfing." This thought-provoking text can be a step toward achieving high levels of energy and well-being.
0-943920-52-3 cloth $19.95

These are only a few of the titles we offer. If you cannot find our books at your local bookstore, you can order directly from us. Call or write for our free catalog:

Metamorphous Press
P.O. Box 10616
Portland, Oregon 97210-0616
(503) 228-4972
or
Toll free 1-800-937-7771

Shipping and handling charges are $2.75 for each book and $.75 for each additional title. We ship UPS unless otherwise requested. Foreign orders please include $1 for each additional book - all orders must be prepaid in U.S. dollars. Please write or call directly to determine additional charges. Prices and availability may change without notice.